EDGE BOOKS™

STARS OF PRO WRESTLING

★ ★ ★ ★ ★ ★ ★ ★ ★

TRIPLE H

BY ANGIE PETERSON KAELBERER

Consultant:
Mike Johnson, Writer
PWInsider.com

CAPSTONE PRESS
a capstone imprint

Edge Books are published by Capstone Press,
151 Good Counsel Drive, P.O. Box 669, Mankato, Minnesota 56002.
www.capstonepub.com

012011
006049R

Books published by Capstone Press are manufactured with paper
containing at least 10 percent post-consumer waste.

Library of Congress Cataloging-in-Publication Data
Kaelberer, Angie Peterson.
    Triple H / by Angie Peterson Kaelberer.
    p. cm. — (Edge books. Stars of pro wrestling)
    Includes bibliographical references and index.
    Summary: "Describes the life and career of pro wrestler Triple H" —
Provided by publisher.
    ISBN 978-1-4296-3948-4 (library binding)
    1. Triple H., 1969– — Juvenile literature. 2. Wrestlers — United States —
Biography — Juvenile literature. I. Title.
GV1196.T75K34 2010
    796.812092 — dc22   2009027262

Editorial Credits
Kathryn Clay, editor; Kyle Grenz, designer; Jo Miller, media researcher;
    Laura Manthe, production specialist

Photo Credits
AP Images/Jon Chase, 12
Getty Images Inc., 9; Kevin Winter, 11; Russell Turiak, 17; WireImage/Bob
    Levey, 25; Djamilla Rosa Cochran, 22;
Globe Photos/Ed Geller/E.G.I., 27; Graham Whitby-Boot/Allstar, cover; John
    B Zissel/IPOL/PHOTOG, 15; John Barrett, 6, 19, 20, 21;
Newscom, 18; Globe Photos/John Barrett, 29; Splash News and Pictures, 5
Wikimedia/Creative Commons/Mshake3, 26

Design Elements
Shutterstock/amlet; Henning Janos; J. Danny; kzww

The author dedicates this book to Dylan Morphis, a true pro wrestling fan.

TABLE OF CONTENTS

Chapter 1

SHOWDOWN IN A CELL

On June 13, 2004, pro wrestling fans filled the Nationwide Arena in Columbus, Ohio. They were there to see Bad Blood, a World Wrestling Entertainment (WWE) event. The last match of the evening was a cell match. Hunter Hearst Helmsley, known as Triple H, would wrestle Shawn Michaels.

The noise inside the arena was deafening as Triple H and Michaels made their way into the ring. A steel cage slowly lowered from the ceiling. Once the wrestlers were in the ring, the cage reached the ground and completely surrounded the men. There would be no escape from the locked cell.

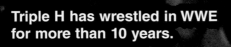

Triple H has wrestled in WWE for more than 10 years.

Triple H attempted to perform a Pedigree on Shawn Michaels.

Triple H opened the match by backing Michaels into a corner. The two traded blows and bodyslams. Then Michaels pushed Triple H's head into the steel cage, leaving him with a bloody forehead.

As the match continued, metal folding chairs, a ladder, and even the steel ring steps became weapons. Triple H lifted the steps and slammed them twice into Michaels' head. He tried to perform his **signature move**, the *Pedigree*, but Michaels kicked out. Then Michaels took control by slamming a chair twice over Triple H's head. As Triple H lay helpless on the mat, Michaels went for the pin. Would Triple H be able to fight back?

signature move — the move for which a wrestler is best known; this move is also called a finishing move.

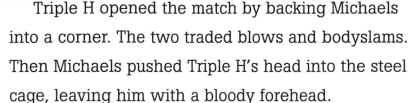

Pedigree — a wrestler holds the opponent face down and drops to his knees, slamming the opponent's head to the mat

Chapter 2

GYM RAT TO WRESTLER

Triple H's real name is Paul Michael Levesque, though many people call him Hunter. He was born July 27, 1969, to Paul Levesque Sr. and Patricia Levesque. He grew up in Nashua, New Hampshire, with his older sister, Lynn.

As a kid, Hunter played baseball and basketball. But his favorite sport was pro wrestling. Hunter and his dad watched wrestling on TV every Saturday and also went to live shows.

WRESTLING FACT

Wrestler Ric Flair was Hunter's hero when he was a kid. From 2003 to 2005, Hunter wrestled with Flair as part of the wrestling group Evolution.

Since he was a teenager, Triple H has worked hard to build his muscles.

Discovering Bodybuilding

At age 14, Hunter was a tall, skinny kid. One day he saw a new gym in Nashua. Hunter walked in and watched the bodybuilders working out. Hunter decided he wanted to build his muscles too. He used his paper route money to pay for a membership at the gym. Soon he spent all of his free time there. The bodybuilders at the gym were older than Hunter. But they helped him with his workouts when they saw how serious he was about bodybuilding.

By age 17, Hunter was 6 feet, 4 inches (1.9 meters) tall and weighed 210 pounds (95 kilograms). He won bodybuilding contests including Teen Mr. New Hampshire. But Hunter didn't want a career as a bodybuilder. He wanted to be a pro wrestler.

King of the Workout

Hunter is one of the most dedicated weightlifters in WWE. His wrestling schedule means that he travels more than 200 days each year. Wherever he goes, Hunter finds a place to work out. One time he even worked out in a shack in Africa!

Hunter says that weightlifting has given him more than a muscular body. He believes it helps him work hard, be disciplined, and not give up when times get tough. These things have all helped him reach the top of the wrestling world.

Walter "Killer" Kowalski (left) trained Hunter.

WRESTLING SCHOOL

At the gym where he worked and trained, Hunter met weightlifter Ted Arcidi. Arcidi had worked as a pro wrestler for a short time. Hunter asked Arcidi to help him get into the wrestling business. At first, Arcidi said no. He knew how tough a wrestler's life could be. But Arcidi couldn't change Hunter's mind. He finally told Hunter about a wrestling school in Malden, Massachusetts. Former wrestler Walter "Killer" Kowalski owned the school.

Hunter started training with Kowalski in 1991. He trained four nights a week while keeping his day job as a gym manager. After a few months of training, Hunter was ready to wrestle.

TERRA RYZING

Kowalski's wrestling company was called the International Wrestling Federation (IWF). The IWF put on small wrestling shows in the northeastern United States. But before Hunter could wrestle, he needed a wrestling name. Most wrestlers make up a name that sounds exciting or tough. Hunter picked the name Terra Ryzing. Soon he was wrestling at shows all over the northeastern United States and Canada. About six months after Hunter started with the IWF, he won his first championship.

Hunter was having fun and learning a lot about the wrestling business. But he was only making about $50 at each match. Hunter knew that if he was going to make a living as a wrestler, he had to join a bigger wrestling company.

World Championship Wrestling

While still working at the gym, Hunter met Chip Burnham, a promoter for World Championship Wrestling (WCW). This large wrestling company was based in Atlanta, Georgia. Hunter gave Burnham a videotape of his best matches. WCW officials viewed the tape and liked what they saw. In 1994, Hunter went to Atlanta for a tryout with WCW. At the end of the tryout, WCW offered him a one-year contract. His salary would be $50,000.

At first, Hunter wrestled as Terra Ryzing in WCW. But WCW officials wanted him to have a new name and personality in the ring. Hunter became Jean-Paul Levesque. His character was a rich, snobby Frenchman. He wrestled with William Regal in a tag team called the Bluebloods.

Vince McMahon (right) was instantly impressed with Hunter's moves.

Hunter was doing OK in WCW, but he wasn't yet a star. He believed that the only way to become a top wrestler would be to work for the World Wrestling Federation (WWF). Today this wrestling company is called World Wrestling Entertainment. Hunter met with WWF owner Vince McMahon. He was thrilled when McMahon offered him a job. Hunter's career was about to take off.

Chapter 3

BECOMING A BIG-TIME HEEL

McMahon gave Hunter a new wrestling name — Hunter Hearst Helmsley. But this character wasn't much different from Jean-Paul Levesque. Hunter's character was still rich and snobby. He wore a **riding habit** into the ring and developed the Pedigree as his signature move.

Hunter was a **heel**. Many wrestlers prefer being **babyfaces**. They want to be cheered by the fans. But Hunter liked acting like a bad guy in the ring. Whatever role he played, he wanted to put on the best possible show for the fans.

In October 1996, Hunter won his first WWF championship. He defeated Marc Mero to become the Intercontinental Champion. In June 1997, Hunter won the King of the Ring tournament.

riding habit — an outfit worn for horseback riding

heel — a wrestler who acts as a villain in the ring

babyface — a wrestler who acts as a hero in the ring

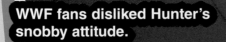

WWF fans disliked Hunter's snobby attitude.

D-GENERATION X

In October 1997, Hunter became part of a wrestling **stable**. He teamed with Shawn Michaels and Chyna to form D-Generation X (DX). Later, wrestlers X-Pac, Billy Gunn, and Road Dogg Jesse James joined them. The DX wrestlers pulled pranks and made jokes. As part of DX, Hunter changed his look. He wore jeans, T-shirts, a leather cap, and sunglasses. Instead of being snobby, he now acted tough in the ring. People started calling him Triple H.

Triple H's tough clothes matched his tough attitude.

Other members of DX included X-Pac (center).

DX started out as a group of heels. But fans liked their pranks and put-downs of other wrestlers. Fans started to cheer DX, and they became babyfaces. But Hunter still preferred being a heel. After two years, Hunter left DX to wrestle on his own.

stable — a group of wrestlers who protect each other during matches and sometimes wrestle together

A True Champion

Triple H had won minor championships, but he hadn't yet moved into the big time. That changed in August 1999. He beat Mankind to win the WWF World Championship. In September, Triple H lost the title to Vince McMahon. He regained it 10 days later by defeating five other wrestlers in a Six-Pack Challenge.

Mankind (left) was one of Triple H's biggest rivals.

Overcoming Injuries

Hunter has had two major injuries during his career. In 2001, he was wrestling Chris Jericho when he tore the quadriceps muscle in his left leg. Hunter was in incredible pain but wanted to finish the match. Once the match was over, an ambulance took him to the hospital. He had an operation to fix the muscle and spent eight months getting back into shape.

In 2007, Hunter tore the quadriceps muscle in his right leg. He had surgery again and took six months off to recover. After both injuries, he came back to win the WWE World Heavyweight Championship.

Chris Jericho (left) put an opponent in the Walls of Jericho during a match at Madison Square Garden.

Evolution members Randy Orton, Batista, and Ric Flair (left to right) wrestled together in 2003.

Early in 2003, Triple H formed another stable. He teamed with Ric Flair, Randy Orton, and Batista to create Evolution. This group of heels ruled WWE for the next two years. At one point in 2003, its members held all of the major WWE titles.

In 2004, Triple H **feuded** with Shawn Michaels, his former DX partner. In January, Michaels challenged Hunter to a Last Man Standing Match. Hunter's World Heavyweight title was on the line. At the end of the match, both wrestlers were knocked out. Triple H got to keep his title, but the feud with Michaels continued. It led to the cell match at Bad Blood in June 2004.

feud — a long-running quarrel between two people or groups of people

Chapter 4

IT'S ALL ABOUT THE GAME

At Bad Blood 2004, Michaels tried for the pin, but Triple H was able to kick out. Then Michaels grabbed a ladder and brought it into the ring. He hit Triple H with it several times before setting it up in the corner. Then Michaels slammed Triple H into the ladder — once, twice, three times!

Triple H staggered out of the ring and grabbed a table, which he set up in the ring. Michaels set Triple H on the table and climbed up the ladder. Using a flying elbow drop, Michaels sent Triple H through the table. Michaels then went for his signature move, *Sweet Chin Music*, but Triple H ducked. He grabbed Michaels and gave him a Pedigree. But Michaels kicked out before the referee counted to three. After both men got to their feet, Triple H gave Michaels two more Pedigrees. Then he pinned Michaels for the win.

Triple H worked hard to become a WWE superstar.

WRESTLING MOVE

Sweet Chin Music — a wrestler kicks an opponent in the chin with the sole of his foot

Dedicated to Wrestling

Some pro wrestlers use their fame to break into show business. But Hunter has said that he eats, sleeps, and breathes the wrestling business. Wrestling announcer Jim Ross called Hunter "the biggest student of the game." Hunter's fans shortened this nickname to "The Game."

WWE announcers Jerry Lawler (left) and Jim Ross (right) call Hunter "The Game."

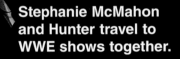

Stephanie McMahon and Hunter travel to WWE shows together.

Even Hunter's family is involved in the wrestling business. In 2003, Hunter married Stephanie McMahon. Stephanie's father is WWE owner Vince McMahon. Stephanie works as a head writer for WWE. Sometimes she even appears on the shows.

Hunter and Stephanie have two daughters. Aurora Rose was born in 2006. Murphy Claire was born in 2008. The two girls travel with their parents to WWE shows across the country.

Hunter works with his wife behind the scenes. He helps set up WWE matches and works with younger wrestlers on their skills. Hunter also likes acting and has appeared in the movie *Blade: Trinity*. But wrestling will always come first for him. His dedication and ability have made him one of the all-time legends of the sport.

WRESTLING FACT

Triple H has won every major WWE title. These titles include the WWF Championship, the World Heavyweight Championship, the Intercontinental Championship, and the Tag Team Championship.

Triple H showed off his championship belt at a WrestleMania press conference in New York.

GLOSSARY ★ ★ ★ ★ ★

babyface (BAY-bee-fayss) — a wrestler who acts as a hero in the ring

bodybuilder (BAH-dee-bil-duhr) — a person who develops muscles through exercise and diet

feud (FYOOD) — a long-running quarrel between two people or groups of people

heel (HEEL) — a wrestler who acts as a villain in the ring

quadriceps (KWAH-druh-seps) — a muscle in the front part of the thigh

riding habit (RYE-ding HAB-it) — an outfit worn for horseback riding

signature move (SIG-nuh-chur MOOV) — the move for which a wrestler is best known; this move is also called a finishing move.

stable (STAY-buhl) — a group of wrestlers who protect each other during matches and sometimes wrestle together

READ MORE ★ ★ ★ ★ ★ ★

O'Shei, Tim. *Shawn Michaels.* Stars of Pro Wrestling. Mankato, Minn.: Capstone Press, 2010.

Shields, Brian, and Kevin Sullivan. *WWE Encyclopedia.* New York: DK Publishing, 2009.

★ ★ INTERNET SITES

FactHound offers a safe, fun way to find Internet sites related to this book. All of the sites on FactHound have been researched by our staff.

Here's all you do:

Visit *www.facthound.com*

FactHound will fetch the best sites for you!

INDEX ★ ★ ★ ★ ★ ★ ★